D0841163

Norway Travel Guide

An Illustrative Guide to Discovering Norway |
With Cultural Insights, Multiple Itineraries,
Detailed maps, Advices from Locals, Planning
Tools & Practical Tips

By

World Citizen

responsibility or blame be held against the publisher for any reparation, damages, or monetary loss due to the information herein, either directly or indirectly.

Respective authors own all copyrights not held by the publisher.

The information herein is offered for informational purposes solely and is universal as such. The presentation of the information is without a contract or any type of guarantee assurance.

The trademarks that are used are without any consent, and the publication of the trademark is without permission or backing by the trademark owner. All trademarks and brands within this book are for clarifying purposes only and are owned by the owners themselves, not affiliated with this document.

Contents

Introduction

Norway is a beautiful country with a wealth of history and culture just waiting to be discovered by visitors. Norway, in the far north of Europe, exemplifies the harmony and beauty of the natural world. Discover the country of the midnight sun and the magnificent aurora borealis with the help of this travel guide.

By following the advice in this guide, you can go from the crowds of the capital city of Oslo to the quiet of the Arctic tundra. Learn the fascinating history of the Vikings, explore the lore of trolls and other fantastical beings, and lose yourself in a world where the past and present coexist in perfect harmony.

The natural beauty of Norway is certain to take your breath away at every turn. Explore the western shore against the stunning backdrop of the fjords that reach out like cold arms. Learn the lesson of humility when you witness the sheer force of waterfalls like the Seven Sisters as they roar into deep valleys.

Norway is home to a number of protected areas where you may see reindeer running free across large stretches of land and listen to the eerie call of the mighty sea eagle reverberating off the mountains. Put on your hiking boots and journey into the unspoiled wilderness, where the lush greenery of the trees, the majesty of the mountains, and the clarity of the lakes will enchant you.

Norway is known for its stunning scenery, but the country also has strong cultural traditions. Explore the historical and cultural treasures of Trondheim, renowned for its many festivals and rich history, or visit the UNESCO World Heritage site of Bryggen in Bergen. Try local favorites like lutefisk and fresh seafood served up in coastal cities.

Norway has something to offer every type of tourist, whether you're an explorer in search of thrills, a nature lover in need of peace and quiet, or a culture vulture in search of undiscovered treasures. Get ready for an adventure of a lifetime through a country that exemplifies the enchantment of nature and human ingenuity by packing your luggage and opening your heart to the delights of Norway with this guide as your compass.

Chapter 1: Planning a Norway Road Trip

The overall coastline of Norway is 25,148 kilometers (15,626 miles), making it a difficult driving destination. The beautiful fjords in the western portion of the nation are undeniably alluring, but there are also the sleepy fishing towns of the southern coast and the rugged islands of the Arctic Ocean to think about. And why would anyone want to miss out on visiting contemporary Oslo and historic Bergen, two of Europe's most intriguing cities? How can one see as many as possible in one action-packed vacation?

1.1 Where Should You Begin Your Trip?

When planning a road trip through Norway, it's important to focus on just one or two regions so that you can see as much of this stunning country as possible. You could drive across the country in a few days, but it would take you at least four days to get to the northernmost point and return. It will cost you a significant penny to return a rental car to a different location in Norway. The western fjords are easily accessible from Bergen, and the southern coast is just a short drive from Oslo, so it's easiest to base yourself in one of these cities and explore a pretty restricted area from there. Bod is an excellent starting point for excursions to the nearby Lofoten Islands.

1.2 How Much Time Should Be Allocated?

Keep in mind that you won't be able to see as much in a day as you could if you were driving at home speeds (the maximum speed limit in Norway is 80 kph or approximately 50 mph) and that highways like those back home are rare. That's because of the winding nature of the country's mountain roads and the narrow paths that hug the shores of its fjords. You could forego looking for the quickest route between two sites in favor of the most aesthetically pleasing one, such as one of Norway's National Tourist Routes. Budget in plenty of wiggle room for a few unplanned snapshots. Many trips necessitate taking a ferry or two, which might add 30 minutes to an hour to your travel time.

1.3 When to Visit

The most predictable summer weather occurs between June and August, so you can expect to share the road with many other people who have the same brilliant idea. If you want to stay near a famous attraction, you should make your reservation early. Beautiful spring weather, with less snow at ground level but plenty in the mountains, makes for excellent spring skiing. Fewer people hit the road in the fall since ski resorts haven't opened and summer attractions have shut down. The winter months are the most challenging because of the short days and freezing temperatures.

1.4 Do Not Forget

Roads might collapse unexpectedly due to flooding, avalanches, or icy conditions, leaving you stranded for hours even though the weather prediction is clear. Keep a watch out for moose, reindeer, and the occasional stray sheep, especially in places you wouldn't think they'd be. Keep in mind that fjord crossings will lengthen your trip. A road trip through Norway can be the experience of a lifetime, but only if you prepare for the unexpected and keep an eye on the weather.

Chapter 2: Discover Norway

2.1 Discover the Whereabouts

2.1.1 Oslo

In recent years, Oslo, the capital of Norway, has shifted its focus to the area along the waterfront that has been underutilized. New areas like Aker Brygge and Tjuvholmen, spurred by the construction of the Oslo Opera House, have transformed the city into one of Europe's liveliest.

2.1.2 Oslofjord

The fjord that gives Oslo its vibrancy also houses Viking relics, walled cities, and bohemian artists' colonies, all of which shed light on the area's rich history.

2.1.3 Svalbard

Only Arctic foxes, Svalbard reindeer, and the elusive polar bears call the cold tundra of Svalbard, located halfway between the continent and the North Pole, home.

2.1.4 Central Norway

This pristine area features some of Europe's highest peaks, making it ideal for winter sports like skiing and snowshoeing. Some of the world's most stunning landscapes are in these national parks.

2.1.5 Bergen

Beautiful Bryggen, a stretch of clapboard buildings facing the dock that harkens back to the country's nautical days, is just one example of how the country's second-largest city honors its history.

2.1.6 Southern Norway

The southernmost part of Norway, often known as Norway's Riviera, is dotted with picturesque fishing villages, many of which date back to the 18th and 19th centuries and are built entirely of wood.

2.1.7 Western Fjords

Cruising the magnificent blue fjords, where the mountains seem to climb at impossible angles, is the greatest way to observe Norway's western coast. The Flåmsbana is a breathtaking train excursion that should not be missed.

2.1.8 Northern Norway

The outstanding northern lights fill the night sky with color in this faraway place. In the summer, it seems like the sun never sets.

2.1.9 Trondheim to the Lofoten Islands

Trondheim, a seaside city, is at the forefront of New Nordic cuisine and has won numerous honors for its efforts. It's ideally situated on the way to some of the most beautiful islands in the country.

2.2 Food and Drink Options in Norway

2.2.1 Skoleboller

Once upon a time, kids' lunches included "school buns" stuffed with custard and sprinkled with shredded coconut. It's great that most cafes stock them, as people with a sweet craving absolutely require them.

2.2.2 Reindeer

When in northern Norway, where the Sámi natives herd reindeer, you simply must try their meat. It's served with mashed potatoes and either cranberry or lingonberry sauce. Sámi National Day is celebrated on February 6th, and the third week of September sees the annual SMAK street food event in Troms. The meat is either dried or processed into sausages and kebabs.

2.2.3 Brown Cheese

Norwegians still regularly use brunost, a tan or brown goat cheese that has a slightly sweet caramelized flavor, in their morning or midday sandwiches and on top of afternoon waffles. Anne Hov, a milkmaid in the 19th century, is credited with inventing it. Restaurant owners often insist that patrons sample dairy products from neighboring farms due to the wide variety of regional variations.

2.2.4 King Crab

In the 1960s, Soviet scientists introduced king crabs to the Barents Sea, where they soon spread to Norway. Norwegian premium dining serves them in soup or with toast and mayonnaise.

2.2.5 Smalahove

If you're in rural western Norway during the holidays, don't be astonished if you find yourself starring at Smalahove – and possibly being stared back. The dish consists of boiled sheep's head (typically without the brain) served with potatoes and mashed rutabaga.

2.2.6 Fish soup

Norway's second-largest city, Bergen, makes a version using halibut, salmon, or shrimp in addition to the cod. It's a warming winter dish.

2.2.7 Pinnekjøtt

Most Norwegian households offer "stick meat"—lamb or mutton ribs with potatoes—on Christmas Eve.

2.2.8 Fish Cakes

Norwegian fish cakes are thinner and served with the potatoes or inside a bun in roadside cafes and on ferries.

2.2.9 Fårikål

In autumn, you must try Norway's unofficial national meal, fårikål, a cabbage and mutton stew. Beer complements stew, which is usually served with bread and potatoes.

2.2.10 Lapskaus

Lapskaus, a stew containing beef or pig, vegetables, and potatoes, originated from northern Germany and spread to Scandinavia and England. Norwegian home cooking's mainstay pairs well with local brews.

2.2.11 Meatballs

Norwegian meatballs, thicker and less spherical than Swedish ones, are another home cuisine favorite eaten with mashed potatoes and brown gravy.

2.2.12 Lefse

Lefse is thin, adaptable potato flatbread. Sugar, butter, and cinnamon are usually placed on it, rolled up, then cut into pieces. Nordland County's brown cheese møsbrømlefse is thicker.

2.2.13 Lutefisk

Lutefisk—"lye fish"—is aged stockfish and lye. The lye-treated gelatinous dish isn't for everyone. Norwegians celebrate it at Christmas. White wine pairs well.

2.2.14 Stockfish

Air-dried cod with potatoes and vegetables is known as stockfish. The dish was developed in northern Norway, namely in the Lofoten Islands, where cod is gathered in the winter and then cured on wooden racks until the following spring.

2.2.15 Ribbe

Ribbe, another Christmastime delicacy, is harder to pass up than lutefisk. After several hours in the oven, this roast pork belly with potatoes, sour cabbage, and lingonberry sauce makes a perfect Christmas supper.

2.3 What to Purchase in Norway

2.3.1 Cloudberry Jam

Cloudberries are rich in vitamin C and have a sweet-and-sour taste like raspberries. The original Sámi people survived severe Arctic winters by eating the fruit.

2.3.2 Caviar Tube

Norwegians love "tube food" because it's easy to carry and doesn't spoil (tubes can be stored at room temperature for two weeks). Caviar, cream cheese, mayonnaise, and other condiments come in tubes.

2.3.3 Troll Figures

Every Norwegian souvenir shop sells troll sculptures in all sizes, shapes, and ugliness! Trolls are part of Norwegian culture; thus, the dolls may seem tacky. Asbjørnsen and Moe, two pals, helped pass down folk tales about them. Norway's Brothers Grimm collected folk tales in the 19th century, including one about Ashlad outwitting a troll. Folk legends characterize the animals as deadly, ugly, and dumb, unlike the smiling, Norwegian-flag-holding, Viking-helmet-adorned souvenir versions.

2.3.4 Akevitt

For your wooden Norwegian cup, try akevitt (aquavit). Norway's potato-based distilled spirit is 40% alcohol by volume and available in clear (aged three to six months) or dark (aged several years) varieties. Other flavors include dill, sweet cumin, cardamom, and others. It's often served together with beer and commonly accompanies authentic Norwegian dishes.

2.3.5 Cheese Slicer

Inspired by his tree slicers, Lillehammer carpenter Thor Bjørklund invented it in the early 20th century. In 1925, he invented the product, which became a major export despite Norwegian cheese makers' attempts to restrict it, fearing it would reduce cheese consumption.

2.3.6 Selbu Mittens

For generations, Norwegians have worn knitwear, and each region has its distinctive patterns. However, the Selbu woolen mitten pattern is famous. Marit Emstad created it 150 years ago at Selbu, near Trondheim. Norway's black-and-white eight-point star mittens are sold everywhere as souvenirs.

2.3.7 Wooden Coffee Mugs

Hikers in Norway may pour coffee from flasks into wooden mugs. Birch mugs are widespread in Norway, Sweden, and Finland, although the Sámi people use reindeer horns. They're outstanding traditional craftsmanship.

2.3.8 Marius Sweaters

Marius, a 1950s sweater pattern, is Norway's most knitted. Marius sweaters are so thick that many wear them without jackets in winter. These pricey sweaters are carefully knit from high-quality wool. Consider them investments because they will last for years if properly maintained.

2.3.9 Kvikk Lunsj

The Norwegian firm Freia's Kvikk Lunsj milk chocolate bar is a lunchbox staple. Like Nestle's KitKat bar, but better, as any Norwegian will tell you! Every supermarket sells Kvikk Lunsj.

2.3.10 Rosemaling Crafts

Artists interested in the country's creative heritage have revived rosemaling, a 19th-century decorative folk painting prevalent in some of the most remote regions. Popular wooden plates, bowls, and vases fit in luggage.

2.3.11 Tomato-Sauced Mackerel

Stavanger, Norway's western oil capital, was a fish-canning center before. The last Norwegian cannery collapsed in 2008, yet canned fish is still a mainstay. Today, mackerel in tomato sauce is popular for lunch, replacing sardines.

Chapter 3: How to Travel Smartly

3.1 What to Bring

A vacation to Norway necessitates a little additional planning when it comes to packing. It pays to dress in layers in a country where the weather is always changing. This is true regardless of the season, whether you're skiing in the towering peaks above Lillehammer in winter or driving along the coastal road near Kristiansand on the hottest summer day.

3.1.1 Clothing

Norway's saying is that bad weather is a bad dress. Prepare for sudden weather changes like the locals. Lightweight athletic undergarments that wick away sweat in summer and thermals in winter make good foundation layers. A wool sweater or fleece jacket is useful year-round because wool is the best insulator. In summer, nighttime temperatures decrease more than expected. If you're going to the mountains or northern coast, your outer layer should be waterproof, windproof, and insulated. In fall, winter, and spring, bring a hat, scarf, and gloves. A sturdy rain jacket and hiking pants are useful all summer long. They're essential for rainy Bergen and the western fjords.

Except for formal occasions, Norwegians dress casually. Even sophisticated eateries allow sweaters. In Norway, a scarf or pashmina dresses up every piece of clothing.

3.1.2 Footwear

Hiking in Norway requires good footwear to avoid catastrophic injury. You need gripping soles on most treks, especially in the mountains, because bare rocks can be slippery when wet. Instead of rain boots, buy a decent pair of waterproof hiking shoes that may be worn in the city. It saves a lot of suitcase room. Most journeys require suitable walking shoes. If it rains, they should be waterproof. Heels are useless on cobblestone streets in towns and in the countryside.

3.1.3 Other Items

No of the season, a daypack that can withstand rain is a need. Don't forget the sunscreen and insect repellent in summer, especially if you'll be spending any time in the mountains. (If the sun decides to make an appearance, it is actually rather powerful, and tourists who aren't prepared often get burned by the sun despite the pleasant breezes and mild temperatures.) You might wish to pack some motion sickness pills if you plan on taking a long boat ride or driving over winding mountain roads. Norway's tap water is free, nutritious, and tastes great, so bringing a reusable water bottle is a great idea.

3.2 Learn Before You Visit

Is seeing the northern lights more appealing to you than the west coast's natural splendor? Are plans in the works to visit other Norwegian cities than Oslo? There are a few things you should know before your trip to Norway so that you can make the most of your stay there.

3.2.1 With a Few Notable Exceptions, Oslo is the Least Stereotypically Norwegian City in the Country

Norway's capital is international, with glittering towers. However, if you know where to look, the city has some of the country's classic architecture. The colorful, wooden 18th- and 19th-century buildings around Damstredet and Telthusbakken in central Oslo are typically Norwegian. The Norsk Folkemuseum in Bygdøy has a stave church and other historical attractions.

3.2.2 A Day Could Bring All Four Seasons to You

Mountain weather in Norway is unpredictable. Regardless of the season, you'll probably get wet or cold. You'll need to bundle up whether you're hiking in the countryside or sightseeing in town. A wicking base layer, a woolen or other knit layer for warmth, and a water- and windproof jacket are ideal. Hiking shoes with high traction are essential on Norway's steep, rocky mountain slopes, so pay attention to your footwear.

3.2.3 In the Winter, not all of Norway is a Wonderland

If you're visiting Stavanger in winter, don't expect a winter wonderland. Western Norway's coastal areas get more rain than snow. The Gulf Stream keeps the fjords from freezing. Snowcapped summits may be visible in the distance. Additionally, Fjord Norway's winter vistas can be seen on year-round fjord excursions.

3.2.4 Eating Out is Costly

To save money, stay in a place with a kitchen. Otherwise, budget 150–400 NKr for dinner. Lunch is usually the cheapest meal, although places vary greatly, so shop around. In restaurants, a noon lunch with drinks costs between NKr 80 and NKr 180, while kiosks and cafés provide sandwiches and pastries for 30–100 NKr. If you choose the latter, ask about specials—most restaurants offer soup or salad with bread for lunch. Off-the-beaten-path restaurants are cheaper regardless of the meal.

3.2.5 Part of Your Food May Come from a Tube

Norwegians enjoy tube food like caviar, mayonnaise, liver pâté, and more in tubes because it's convenient! Norwegians carry sandwiches for work, hiking, and skiing. Tube food doesn't need tools to spread and lasts forever if kept airtight. You might find bacon or shrimp-flavored cream cheese tubes at your hotel's breakfast buffet. So squeeze!

3.2.6 Know When to Talk to Strangers

Norwegians are polite and reserved—perhaps even shy. City residents prefer solitude to little chat. Indeed, on public transit, all the window seats are taken, and people prefer to stand rather than sit next to someone they don't know (until the vehicle gets busy). However, in the mountains, strangers are often greeted and talked to, possibly while helping fellow hikers.

3.2.7 Do Not Be Afraid to Visit in Winter

Norway is great in winter. If you layer, it's not as cold as you think. Flights and hotels are cheaper than in summer. In places like Stavanger and Bergen, where there are only six hours of daylight in December, and Arctic Tromsø, which has no sunlight due to the polar night, you have to plan ahead for road trips and outdoor sightseeing. If you like museums and cafés, Norway's bustling cities are great winter getaways. Additionally, Tromsø's blue twilight between November and January is unforgettable.

3.2.8 You Cannot See Everything in a Week

Instead of trying to see the north, west, and south in one trip, stick to one area and appreciate Norway more. The northern Lofoten Islands, west coast fjords, hiking trails, stave churches, and cities like Stavanger, Bergen, and Ålesund take a week to explore. The 300,000 square kilometers of mountains and fjords make travel difficult.

(Domestic flights to major locations are pricey.) Norway is best explored slowly. Pick a regional base and explore it and its surroundings by rental vehicle or bus/train—you'll be astonished at how many hidden gems you'll find!

3.3 Finding Your Way Around

The government of Norway has made significant strides in recent years to enhance public transportation. The timing of buses, trains, and boats has been meticulously planned to ensure a smooth journey. For example, your train should arrive just before your ferry leaves. Check with local tourist information centers for the most up-to-date schedule information, as operating hours change with the seasons.

3.3.1 Air

Norway's largest airport is Gardermoen Airport, northeast of Oslo. Some long-distance flights land at Bergen Airport, 18 kilometers (11 miles) south of the city. Kristiansand, Tromsø, Sandefjord, Stavanger, and Trondheim also have international airports. These airports only receive Norwegian and European flights.

New York-Oslo flights last eight hours. Nonstop flights from London take 13/4 hours. American, Delta, and United fly to Oslo. Norwegian Airlines and SAS fly direct from New York and Los Angeles to Oslo and link to northern Europe. European budget airlines EasyJet, Ryanair, and Wizz Air fly to Oslo.

Norwegian Airlines, SAS, and Widerøe, which serve 42 Norwegian destinations, offer many domestic flights. Budget and regional airlines may land at Torp Airport near Sandefjord, 110 kilometers (68 miles) south of Oslo.

Most of the country's airports are controlled by state-owned Avinor. Parking, transfers, and arrivals are on its website.

Airport transfers

Oslo and Bergen airports are easy to reach. Flybussen buses leave arriving terminals for downtown locations often. Bergen Light Rail and Flytoget express trains leave every 10 minutes for Byparken Station and Oslo Central Station, respectively.

3.3.2 Boat & Ferry

Norway has many boating options. Hurtigruten, a coastal ship that has called at 34 Norwegian ports since 1893, is the crown gem. The firm calls the complete journey "the world's most beautiful sea voyage," departing daily from Bergen in the southwest and heading north to Kirkenes at the Finnish and Russian borders. It then makes the return trip back to Bergen. The 2,500-nautical-mile voyage takes 12 days. Onboard are accommodations, restaurants, cafeterias, and stores. Hurtigruten sells whole-stretch and leg tickets.

Boats can go elsewhere. Western Norway's fjords are popular routes. These include slow-moving ferries and speedboats that let you feel the wind. Other ferries run from Oslo to the charming coastal settlements around Oslofjord, the vast river that reaches the capital.

Don't be shocked if a beautiful fjord road finishes at a ferry port. Norway's west coast and north depend on ferries, making them enjoyable and crucial. Car and passenger ferries connect areas. Due to limited driving space, popular crossings like Lauvvik–Lysebotn have summer waits, so arrive early. Book tour ferries on picturesque routes like Geiranger–Hellesylt in advance.

Oslo has ferry services to the UK, Sweden, Denmark, and Germany. Color Line visits Kiel and Hirtshals, Denmark. Helsingborg-Copenhagen is DFDS Scandinavian Seaways' route.

3.3.3 Bus

Explore Norway's smaller regions by bus. The national railway subsidiary Nettbuss operates many local bus routes to most places. Nor-Way Bussekspress can arrange any trip.

The main bus terminal close to Oslo Central Station has many long-distance buses that may take you to most Norwegian destinations. However, the good train system is slightly more expensive and gives far larger coverage and quicker travel times.

3.3.4 Car

Norway is ideal for long-distance drivers. Norway's National Tourist Routes are 18 breathtaking country drives. These coastal routes span over 1,850 kilometers (1,150 miles). A car journey around the western fjords is an excellent way to see the region, as more than half are there. The Rondane National Tourist Route and Lofoten Islands National Tourist Route are fantastic alpine drives.

Southern Norway's major cities are all within a day's travel. Routes follow the southern coastline with a moderate curve. Norway narrows as it crosses Sweden, Finland, and the Arctic Circle to touch Russia. For safety, plan ahead in distant places, notably northern Norway, where road conditions can change. If your road trip crosses mountains in winter, autumn, or spring, be sure the mountain pass is open. Some high mountain roads close in October due to snow and reopen in June.

Only major cities have four-lane freeways. Outside key routes, roads are small and winding with few guardrails. Summer roadways are always congested. Directional, distance, and informational signs line Norwegian roadways. Right-hand drive. Allow right-turning cars.

Falck Global Assistance and Norges Automobil-Forbund offer roadside assistance.

Road Rules

You can get behind the wheel in Norway with a valid license from the United States, Canada, the United Kingdom, Australia, or New

Zealand. Some cities in Norway, including Oslo, Bergen, Trondheim, Stavanger, and Kristiansand, require payment to access. Gray metal boxes equipped with radar and cameras patrol most highways. Many roadways have warning signs about ATMs installed at regular intervals. Always use your headlights and fasten your seat belts to stay safe on the road.

3.3.5 Cruise Ship

The most beautiful and famous fjords in Norway are on the west coast, and coastal cruises are the best and most pleasant way to see them. Cruises normally offer at least one excursion in each port, usually a walk or bus trip, so you may get an overview of each port and pay for more extensive touring or fun activities.

Most major cruise lines—Norwegian, Celebrity, Princess, Holland America, and Costa Cruises—offer coastal cruises. Viking, with cruises from Bergen to Honningsvåg, is the most luxurious.

3.3.6 Train

Norway features world-class rail rides. The Flåmsbana, which runs 20 km (12 miles) from Myrdal to Flåm, is a tourist route, but many of them are commercial routes that pass through beautiful landscapes. The Bergensbanen from Oslo to Bergen is famous. 180 tunnels, lakes, streams, and mountains await you on the seven-hour ride to Finse Station.

Norway's longest rail line stretches north from Trondheim to Fauske and Bodø. The picturesque western line crosses Hardangervidda between Oslo and Bergen, while the southern line follows the coast to Stavanger. Flying is commonly necessary to travel from south to north in Norway, as Stavanger is as close to Rome as it is to the north.

3.4 Essentials

3.4.1 Dining

Nordic food has much to offer. Local, sustainable products, novel cooking methods, and forest produce make meals special. Local specialties include roast reindeer, fresh-caught salmon and shrimp, and a variety of orchard fruits. Bergen, Stavanger, and Trondheim also have good eating. Only expensive prices make it hard to indulge.

Norwegians still eat their grandparents' meals. Fårikål and lutefisk, childhood favorites, are more popular than ever, especially during the holidays. These and other typical dishes are likely on the menu at any restaurant that advertises them. Visit the bakeries—pastries are popular here.

Norwegian kitchens are open from lunchtime to 10 or 11 pm. Sunday eateries are closed. Even in tiny towns, kebabs and pizza shops are open late.

Free breakfasts at hotels range from pastries and coffee to elaborate buffets. Few hotels include afternoon tea or a light meal in the room rate. Most hotels feature restaurants.

3.4.2 Lodging

Norway has many accommodations. Most high-end restaurants are regional and international chains, while some are independent and family-owned. Small guesthouses, pensions, and B&Bs offer more personalized service.

During winter, luxury ice hotels and igloos are growing increasingly popular. Book a fisherman's hut on the coast. Tourist bureaus can book these accommodations. Norway offers around 1,000 tent campgrounds. The Norwegian Trekking Association maintains several hiking trail shelters, some with service.

Non-backpacker hostels are popular. Many have family rooms.

Facilities

If a delicious breakfast is a must, research hotels before booking. Some charge for a packaged lunch or small meal. Guesthouses and hostels usually offer rooms with common and private bathrooms.

Parking

Some hotels offer free parking, while others charge. Winter underground parking is better to start your car and avoid ice and snow.

Prices

Seasonal lodging prices vary. During the northern lights season, hotels charge more, but summer offers are common. Weekend prices are higher.

Reservations

Due to extreme weather, winter and summer reservations are suggested. Book early for scenic rooms.

3.4.3 Health and Safety

Norway's healthcare is world-class. Drugstores, supermarkets, and petrol stations sell painkillers and other drugs. Cities have at least one nighttime drugstore.

The sun is intense, even in cool temperatures. Wear long pants and bright garments to notice ticks in forest regions, especially along the southern coast from Oslo to Trondheim. Pharmacy tweezers can remove ticks immediately.

3.4.4 Passports

For stays up to three months, all U.S. citizens, including infants, must have a passport. You may be denied entrance if your passport expires three months after your trip.

3.4.5 Money

Norway, a non-EU country, kept its currency when its neighbors adopted the euro. NKr represents the Norwegian crown. Price tags usually read "Kr" followed by the amount.

3.4.6 Telephones

Norway's country code is 47. No area codes—dial all eight numbers of any phone number. Mobile phones with 9 or 4 prefixes are more expensive. 82-prefixed numbers cost more. 800/810 numbers are toll-free. 815 calls cost NKr 1.

3.4.7 Packing

Pack layers for sudden weather changes. In winter, long underwear, wool socks, and a windproof jacket protect you from severe chills, while a rain jacket or umbrella is useful for sudden rainstorms. Hike with long-sleeved shirts and pants to avoid ticks. Sunscreen and a hat are essential in the sun. Bring button-down shirts to supper.

3.4.8 Tipping

Wages in Norway are far greater than in other countries; tipping is not commonly practiced. However, a 10% gratuity is customary while dining out, especially at fancier restaurants. Taxi drivers do not anticipate tips, although a ten-cent increase is always welcomed.

3.5 When to Visit

Low Season: Northern Norway nevertheless sees a significant amount of traffic from aurora borealis-chasers in November and December, despite it being the off-season. Be aware that several routes and mountain passes close from October until the end of May due to the extreme cold and darkness that characterizes winter. There are also closures of several attractions.

Shoulder Season: Avoid the heat and humidity by visiting in the shoulder seasons of April through May and September through October. It's possible, up north, to witness the midnight sun in May or the northern lights in October. But hotels don't lower their prices.

High Season: From June through August, Norway is overrun with tourists. Travel arrangements and hotel rooms are typically reserved well in advance. It's essential to prepare for both rain and shine by bringing along clothing. Skiing, snowmobiling, and even dogsledding are all enjoyable throughout the winter months of January through March.

3.6 Important Contacts

3.6.1 Air

Airlines

Norwegian Airlines. P 21–49–00–15 w www.norwegian.com.

Widerøe. P 75–80–35–68 w www.wideroe.no.

Scandinavian Airlines. P 21–89–64–00 w www.flysas.com.

Airport Transfers

Flytoget. P 23–15–90–00 w flytoget.no/en.

Flybussen. P 48–28–05–00 w www.flybussen.no.

Torp Express Buss. P 23–00–24–00 w
www.torp.no/en/transport/bus.

Airports

Bergen Airports. P 67–03–15–55 w www.airport-bergen.com.

Trondheim Airport. P 67–03–25–00 w
avinor.no/en/airport/trondheim-airport.

Kristiansand Airport. P 67–03–03–30
avinor.no/en/airport/kristiansand-airport.

Tromsø Airport. P 67–03–46–00 w avinor.no/en/airport/tromso-
airport.

Sandefjord Airport. P 33–42–70–00 w www.torp.no/en.

3.6.2 Bus

Contacts

Nor-Way Bussekspress. P 02–231–3150 www.nor-way.no.
Nettbuss. P 04–070–5070 www.nettbuss.no.

Lavprisekspressen. P 06–798–0480 w www.lavprisekspressen.no.

3.6.3 Boat

Contacts

Colorline. P 99–56–19–00 w www.colorline.com/denmark-
Norway.

Hurtigruten. P 810–30–000 w www.hurtigruten.com.

DFDS Scandinavian Seaways. Oslo P 23–10–68–00 w www.dfds.no.

3.6.4 Train
Contacts

Interrail. P 880–0161–05 www.interrail.eu.

Entur. P 06/127–9088 w www.entur.org.

3.6.5 Car
Contacts

Falck Global Assistance. P 21–49–24–15 www.falck.no.

3.6.6 U.S. Embassy/Consulate
Contacts

Royal Norwegian Embassy. 2720 34th Street NW, Washington, D.C. P 202/333–6000 www.norway.no/en/usa.

US Embassy in Norway. Morgedalsvegen 36 P 21–30–85–40 www.no.usembassy.gov.

3.6.7 Visitor Information
Contacts

Norway National Parks. www.nasjonalparkriket.no/en.

Fjord Norway. Stavanger w fjordnorway.com.

Visit Norway. www.visitnorway.com.

Chapter 4: Exploring Norway's Culture and Sites

4.1 Top Experiences in Norway

Every tourist's bucket list should include a visit to Norway for its fantastic attractions. Check out Fodor's best recommendations for an amazing vacation.

4.1.1 Visit Bryggen

The colorful Hanseatic wharf structures in Bergen are a UNESCO World Heritage Site with a rich history.

4.1.2 Explore Svalbard

Longyearbyen, Svalbard's main town, has many restaurants, hotels, cafés, and pubs for its 2,000 residents.

4.1.3 Cruise the Coast

Hurtigruten's former post and freight boats are now luxurious cruise ships that take you on wonderful voyages.

4.1.4 Experience the Northern Lights

Between September and March, millions visit Tromsø to see the northern lights.

4.1.5 Cross-Country Skiing

Lillehammer, the 1994 Winter Olympics host, is a great spot to learn cross-country skiing.

4.1.6 Stavanger's Old Town

Old Stavanger, with 173 18th- and 19th-century wooden buildings, is worth a half-hour stroll.

4.1.7 The Kjerag Boulder

The 12½-mile round-trip climb to Kjerag's boulder is for experienced hikers who want to push themselves.

4.1.8 The Midnight Sun

From late April until late August, the sun never sets in Longyearbyen.

4.1.9 Visit Geirangerfjord

Geiranger, Norway's most famous fjord and a UNESCO World Heritage Site, inspired Frozen's Arendelle.

4.1.10 Drive Trollstigen Road

Western Norway's Trollstigen, or "troll's footpath," is notable for its 11 hairpin twists.

Go Whale-Watching

Herring schools visit Trom's county fjords from November to January. Whales—especially orcas and humpbacks—follow herring.

4.1.11 The North Cape

Magerøya's North Cape is the continent's northernmost. Summer's midnight sun illuminates the photo opportunities.

4.1.12 Take Flåmsbanen.

The exhilarating train trip between Flåm and Myrdal offers stunning mountain vistas.

4.1.13 Try Brown Cheese

Norwegian brown cheese is caramel-flavored and prepared from whey, cream, and cow and goat milk.

4.1.14 The Lofoten Islands

This Arctic archipelago's mountains, fjords, rough coastlines, sandy beaches, and agriculture resemble Norway.

4.1.15 See the Royals

Annually, the royals attend several Norwegian festivals and celebrations. They're humble.

4.1.16 Polar Night

In northern Norway, the sun doesn't rise for four weeks to four months.

4.1.17 Cabin Night

The Lofoten Islands and Geiranger-Ålesund route provide the most picturesque cabin accommodations.

4.1.18 Opera House Rooftop Relaxation

Oslo has several popular hangouts, but few boast the Opera House's rooftop vistas.

4.1.19 Cable Car Ride

Fjellheisen cable cars in Tromsø are among the best in Norway's fjords and mountains.

4.1.20 Hike Pulpit Rock

If you dare glance down, the narrow terrace about 1,970 feet above Lysefjord offers breathtaking vistas. (Ch. 5)

4.1.21 Hike to Trolltunga

One of Norway's best mountain panoramas awaits hikers who can complete the 131-mile round-trip.

4.1.22 Discover the Stave Churches

28 of Norway's outstanding early medieval churches remain. Borgund Stave Church is well-preserved.

4.1.23 Art Nouveau in Ålesund

Norwegians and tourists love Ålesund's Art Nouveau structures, erected after a 1904 fire devastated most of the city center.

4.2 Natural Wonders to Visit in Norway

4.2.1 Sognefjord

Sognefjord is Norway's deepest and longest (127 miles). Its 12 fjords, including Naerøyfjord, a UNESCO World Heritage Site, and Aurlandsfjord, home to the picturesque Flåm Railway, are spectacular.

4.2.2 Marmorslottet

Although few tourists know about it, you should stop by Marmorslottet (Marble Castle) on your way to Svartisen Glacier, which is less than an hour's drive from Mo I Rana. Given its glacial origins, the water is a deep, ice blue.

4.2.3 Svartisen

Svartisen, Norway's second-largest glacier, is accessible despite its Arctic location. One big formation has split into two halves, one west and one east. The glacier reaches about 5,300 feet above sea level.

4.2.4 Hardangervidda

Hardangervidda, Europe's greatest high-altitude plateau (nearly 3,300 square miles), averages 3,600 feet. It is part of the largest Nordic national park, running from western to eastern Norway over Hordaland, Buskerud, and Telemark.

4.2.5 Jotunheimen National Park

Hikers, climbers, and skiers love Jotunheimen. Northern Europe's highest mountain, 8,100-foot Galdhøppingen, is in its 1,300 square miles.

4.2.6 Dovrefjell National Park

Dovre and Dovrefjell-Sunndalsfjella national parks cover 770 square kilometers in southeastern Norway. Wild reindeer and Norway's only wild musk ox, introduced from Greenland in the early 20th century, live there. Safaris brings you near to these Titans.

4.2.7 Jostedalsbreen

Jostedalsbreen is the largest glacier in Norway and continental Europe. Its multitudes of branches cover about 200 square miles. Briksdalsbreen, near Olden, is a popular spot for guided buggy tours.

4.2.8 Gloppedalsura

Gloppedalsura's lunar environment has stones the size of vehicles and houses. They're the remains of northern Europe's greatest rockslide. Gloppedalsura is part of the Magma Geopark because magma created this granite.

4.2.9 Vettisfossen

Europe's tallest unregulated waterfall is the 900-foot Vettisfossen. Vettisfossen, located in Jotunheimen National Park, is only accessible from Utladalen through a steep 71/2.5-mile round-trip climb.

4.2.10 Saltstraumen

Bodø's Saltstraumen boasts the world's strongest tidal current. The narrow, 492-foot-wide, 2-mile-long strait between mainland Norway and Straumøya channels massive amounts of seawater between high and low tides.

4.2.11 Jostedalsbreen

Jostedalsbreen is the largest glacier in Norway and continental Europe. Its multitudes of branches cover about 200 square miles. Briksdalsbreen, near Olden, is a popular spot for guided buggy tours.

4.3 Oslo's Art Attractions

4.3.1 Munch Museum

The Munch Museum is devoted to Norwegian expressionist painter Edvard Munch, widely known for The Scream. This iconic picture was stolen in 2004 and recovered.

4.3.2 Kragstøtten

Kragstøtten refers to both a panoramic view of Oslo and the on-site statue of Hans Hagerup Krag, a 19th-century Norwegian road commissioner. Krag built the roads in the hilltop Holmenkollen neighborhood of northeastern Oslo, which currently houses the ski jump and ski museum.

4.3.3 Vigelandsparken

Due to its collection of 20th-century Gustav Vigeland sculptures, Frognerparken in central Oslo is known as Vigelandsparken. His 212 granite and bronze sculptures dot the huge grounds. The 46-foot life-cycle monument is the highlight.

4.3.4 Peer Gynt Sculpture Park

The Peer Gynt Sculpture Park in northeastern Oslo is named after Norwegian playwright and poet Henrik Ibsen's play of the same name. The park's 20 sculptures, designed by a variety of modern artists, illustrate the plot act by act.

4.3.5 The Tiger

The 15-foot-long bronze tiger in front of Oslo's central train station may be the city's most photographed sculpture. The 2000 city's 1,000th anniversary was commemorated by Norwegian exotic animal sculptor Elena Engelsen.

4.3.6 Ekeberg's Sculpture Park

Ekeberg Sculpture Park, east of central Oslo, combines art and nature. Its 40-plus sculptures incorporate the scenery.

4.3.7 Tjuvholmen Sculpture Park

Tjuvholmen Sculpture Park near Frogner uses Oslo's spectacular scenery—the fjord—like Ekeberg. The park features seven contemporary sculptures designed by Renzo Piano and in collaboration with Denmark's Louisiana Museum of Modern Art.

4.3.8 Holmenkollen Troll

The Kollentrollet (Holmenkollen Troll) is in Holmenkollen. The 23-foot concrete figure is easily found in the woods. Nils Aas, who created King Haakon VII's sculpture on Oslo's 7 June Square, designed him.

4.3.9 Vippa

The Vippa food court, located in a disused warehouse near the Vippetangen port and the Oslofjord, features street food from all over the world, from Norway to Eritrea, Syria to China. The façade is particularly appealing, thanks to a mural depicting significant sites in the capital.

4.3.10 The National Museum

The National Museum is Norway's public art, architecture, and design collection, displaying specimens of art and design from antiquity to the present.

4.4 Norwegian Events and Festivals

4.4.1 January

Polar Night Half-Marathon: This half-marathon occurs on a day when the sun never rises in the Arctic city of Troms during the first week of January. The northern lights, if you're lucky, might be visible.

Visit www.msm.no/en/arrangement/morkertidslopet or call (77)67-33-63.

Festival of the Northern Lights: Jazz, opera, and chamber music are also featured at this classical music festival in Troms.

Contact: P 92-09-32-52 www.nordlysfestivalen.no/en

Tromsø International Film Festival: During the third week of January, people can watch movies from all over the world at the northernmost film festival in the world.

Tel: +47 77 775 30 90 tiff.no/en

4.4.2 February

Sámi National Day: The Sápmi (Lapp) people commemorate their culture on February 6. This territory includes sections of northern Norway, Sweden, Finland, and Russia. Troms hosts a week-long festival that features events including reindeer racing and a lasso-throwing competition.

Call (77) 673-33-63, or check out www.msm.no/en/arrangement/samisk-uke

Ice Music Festival: All musical instruments, from ice cellos to ice drums, is constructed entirely out of ice for this yearly event that takes place at the start of the month.

www.icemusicfestivalnorway.no

Holmenkollmarsjen: The Holmenkoll March is a cross-country ski race held just north of Oslo in the middle of February.

Visit

www.skiforeningen.no/en/kursogarrangement/holmenkollmarsje n or call (022) 92-32-00.

Røros Winter Fair: This huge outdoor market has been going strong since 1854, and every year at the end of February, it attracts 80 horse-drawn sleighs from all over the region.

Call 72–41–00–00 www.rorosmartnan.no

4.4.3 March

Borealis: Midway through March, Bergen hosts an experimental music festival that also features art shows and movie screenings.

Call (95) 90-53-76 or check out www.borealisfestival.no

Birkebeinerrennet: Starting in Rena during the third week of the month, this cross-country ski event concludes in Lillehammer.

Telephone: (41) 77-29-00; Website: birkebeiner.no/en/ski/birkebeinerrennet-54-km

Finnmarksløpet: Beginning in the middle of March, this dogsled race crosses the entirety of northern Norway.

Finnmarkslopet.no, (901) 900-81-519.

4.4.4 April

Easter in the Sámi calendar: The Sámi people gather annually at Karasjok to celebrate their culture with events, including ice fishing contests and reindeer races.

Call 93–22–94–94 www.samieasterfestival.com

4.4.5 May

Bergen International Festival: The Bergen International Festival is a two-week-long celebration of the performing arts.

Call 55–21–06–30 www.fib.no/en

Norwegian National Day: The 17th of May is a national holiday in Norway, marked by parades, hot dogs, and ice cream.

www.visitnorway.com/typically-norwegian/norways-national-day

4.4.6 June

Midnight Sun Marathon: This race, held on a night when the sun doesn't set, is sponsored by the city of Tromsø in the Arctic.

Dial (77) 67-33-63 or visit www.msm.no/en for further information.

Glad Mat: In the last week of June, Stavanger hosts Norway's largest street food festival, which attracts an estimated 250,000 visitors.

To contact, please dial: 51-87-45-78 or visit www.gladmat.no

Festspillene Nord-Norge: Harstad hosts the largest cultural festival in northern Norway.

P 77–04–12–30 festspillnn.no

Sankthansaften: On the evening of June 23 (Saint John's Eve), Norwegians light bonfires and celebrate with the greatest enthusiasm in Iesund.

www.visitnorway.com/media/news-from-norway/sankthans-finds-norway-at-its-brightest-and-most-ummery

4.4.7 July

Riddu Riddu: Midway through July, the Lyngen Alps, not far from Troms, play host to the indigenous culture and music event known as Riddu Riddu.

Contact (971) 39-493 Visit: riddu.no/en

Moldejazz: Moldejazz, held during the fourth week of June in Norway's western fjords, is the country's largest jazz festival.

Tel: +47 71 20 31 50 www.moldejazz.no/en

4.4.8 August

Norwegian International Film Festival: This festival, which takes place at the end of August in Haugesund, is where winners of the coveted Amanda Award are announced.

www.filmfestivalen.no

Parkenfestivalen: During the third week of August, Bodø hosts a festival that attracts performers from all over the world. Visit www.parkenfestivalen.no or call 978-96-486.

4.4.9 September

NuArt: Stavanger hosts Norway's one and only street art festival every September.

www.nuartfestival.no

Marathon in Oslo: Between the last weekend in September and the first weekend in October, 20,000 people go to Norway for the country's largest marathon.

Contact 900–47–200 oslomaraton.no/en

SMAK: Each year in the middle of September, the city of Tromsø hosts a festival to celebrate the cuisine of northern Norway.

www.smakfest.no/en

4.4.10 October

Dark Season Blues Festival: For four months, the sun doesn't rise in Svalbard; therefore at the end of October, the inhabitants like to have a big party to bid farewell to the light.

www.svalbardblues.com

4.4.11 November

Pepperkakebyen Bergen: Bergen, Norway, is the site of Norway's largest gingerbread hamlet.

www.pepperkakebyen.org

4.4.12 December

Christmas Market Røros: A winter wonderland takes over this World Heritage Site.

P 72–41–00–00 julemarkedroros.no

Chapter 5: Oslo

5.1 Top Reasons to Visit

A cause for shouting: Oslo is a city full of artistic and literary treasures, from Munch to Ibsen to Snøhetta to Knausgaard, and there are more and more locations to enjoy them opening up every year.

A Bridge between Old and New Nordic: Chefs have sparked a culinary revolution by championing regional ingredients and experimenting with forward-thinking techniques like New Nordic and waste-free cooking.

Roads always end up in the nature: Without leaving the heart of the capital, you may explore woods, fjords, and unmatched landscapes.

Join the Vikings and other explorers on their voyages: Explore the magnificent ships and boats that our ancestors utilized on their travels, learn about their adventures, and glance at the riches they buried along the way.

Save the planet: With its environmentally friendly public transportation, hotels, and restaurants, Oslo was named the "Eco Capital" of Europe.

Stunning natural beauty, rather than cultural traditions or world-famous institutions, is what truly sets Oslo different from other European towns. How many other global hubs provide direct subway access to a forest, lake, or hiking trail? Norwegians, however, will be the first to point out that the city also boasts a lively nightlife on par with the rest of Scandinavia's major metropolises, as well as world-class cultural institutions and restaurants that draw visitors from all over the globe.

5.2 Sentrum

Downtown Oslo is tiny, featuring shops, museums, historic buildings, restaurants, and clubs in a walkable, beautifully lit center. Some streets are quieter due to the growing diversifying population, while others are busier. The Royal Palace, Parliament Building, and most historic structures are here. The National Museum complex, Munch Museum, and Viking Museum are also located here.

Finding Your Way Around

Oslo is compact and easy to navigate, although its hills make walking or biking harder than in Copenhagen. However, an Oslo Pass lets you ride buses, trains, trams, and the subway between areas. Trams carry USB chargers and are rarely crowded.

Safety

Even though Oslo is one of the world's safest capitals, don't wander alone at night. Though drowsy, you're in a capital city and metropolis.

5.2.1 Sights

1. Nasjonalmuseet (National Museum)

The Nordic region's largest art museum, the National Museum, was inaugurated in 2022. A rooftop hall longer than the Royal Palace overlooks Oslo City Hall, Akershus Fortress, and the Oslofjord in the striking modern building near the waterfront. The Edvard Munch section includes The Dance of Life, one of two oil versions of The Scream, and other self-portraits. Bridal Voyage on the Hardangerfjord by Hans Gude and Adolph Tidemand hangs beside other Norwegian masterworks. Monet, Van Gogh, Renoir, and Gauguin, as well as 20th-century Nordic art, are in the museum. Enjoy year-round events and garden sitting.

Nationaltheatret, Brynjulf Bulls p.l. 3, Sentrum P. 21-98-20-00, www.nasjonalmuseet.no.

2. Nationaltheatret (National Theater)

Henrik Ibsen and Bjørnstjerne Bjørnson, who wrote the national song, are sculptures in front of this 1899 Neoclassical theater. Norwegian dominates performances. A pre-booked English-language tour of the inside costs NKr 90 and explains how famous writers constructed this area.

Please visit www.nationaltheatret.no or write to National Theatret, Johanne Dybwads Pl 1, Sentrum P 22-00-14-00, Norway.

3. Oslo Domkirke (Oslo Cathedral)

Since 1697, Oslo's primary church has been this dark-brown brick edifice, Oslo's third cathedral. Acanthus-carved pulpit, altarpiece, and organ front remain. Look at Hugo Louis Mohr's 1936–1950 ceiling murals and Emanuel Vigeland's stained-glass windows. Visit the bell tower's 19th-century fire department lookout. Pre-book tours.

Karl Johans gt. 11, Sentrum P 23-62-90-10, kirken.no.

4. Rådhuset (City Hall)

Today, this boxy brick edifice is best recognized for awarding the Nobel Peace Prize on December 10. Inside, many museum-quality treasures hang. The royal portraits are upstairs in the Banquet Hall after viewing the Main Hall frescoes. The main hall hosts free 45-minute tours in June and July. Enter City Hall Gallery harborside. Year-round special displays. 60 huge spotlights illuminate the Central Hall outside on festive occasions.

Sentrum P 23-46-12-00, Rdhusplassen 1, https://www.oslo.kommune.no/radhuset/#gref

5. Slottet (The Royal Palace)

The vanilla-and-cream Neoclassical palace was finished in 1848 near Karl Johan Gate. Karl Johan, monarch of Sweden and Norway from 1818 until 1844, is the equestrian statue out front. In summer, English-language guided tours are available at the palace. Attend the 11 am Palace Chapel Sunday service.

Address: Slottsplassen 1, Sentrum P 81-53-31-33 www.kongehuset.no Tickets in advance are NKr 165, and any leftover tickets will be sold at the door for NKr 125.

5.2.2 Restaurants
1. J2

This minimalist modern Korean kitchen in Sentrum has made ripples since opening a few years ago. The mains range from gourmet to comfort food, and the snacks are just as popular. A magnificent dining area, Korean food, and a convenient location.

Average main: NKr200 Pilestredet 63A, Sentrum www.j2restaurant.no/.

2. Kafeteria August

The crew behind Maaemo's casual yet sophisticated food serves it off Tullinlokka Park near the National Gallery. Light, beautiful decor, and minimalism define this 2022 all-day diner. Known for: finest local foods; casual elegant atmosphere; sunny and low key.

Average main: NKr150 Universitetsgata 9, Sentrum P 920-25-580 kafeteriaaugust.no/.

3. Kaffistova

At this simple restaurant on the ground level of Hotell Bondeheimen, Norwegian home cooking is provided. Raspeballer (potato dumplings), boknafisk (dried and salted cod), and rømmegrøt (sour cream porridge) are constantly available. Known for: open-faced shrimp sandwiches, handmade meatballs, and desserts.

Hotell Bondeheimen, Rosenkrantz gt. 8, Sentrum P 23-21-41-00, www.kaffistova.com, average main course NKr180.

4. Katla

This odd restaurant, named for an Icelandic volcano, serves Nordic, Asian, Latin American, and other cuisines. Cooking is done on gas grills or hot lava stones. Small, shareable servings; seafood is the star; always busy, so book early.

Universitetsgata 12, Sentrum P 22-69-50-00, averaging NKr895 as the main entrance. www.katlaoslo.no No Sunday or Monday Hours. There is no midday break during the week.

5. Mamma Pizza

This little osteria serves famed sourdough pizzas and boasts Emilia-Romagna-style checkered tablecloths and striped awning. While you wait, the restaurant serves refreshing yet strong drinks or classic aperitifs and the city's best pie. Short walk from the central railway station; don't miss the dessert of the day; gluten-free dough.

Dronningens gt. 22 in the Sentrum, for instance, has an average main for NKr180.

6. Pink Fish Grensen

This clever, low-key restaurant wants the world to eat more fish. Hot pots, fish-and-chips, and poké bowls are favorites. Famous for: international menu, fast stop on a busy day.

Average main: NKr120 Grensen 17, Sentrum P 45-85-50-27 www.pinkfish.no The Sun is closed.

7. Palmen Restaurant

The Grand Cafe receives all the attention, but the Grand Hotel's more casual—but still rather beautiful—lobby restaurant is the stuff of Bohemian dreams, with marble, gold, crystal, & velvet providing a sumptuous touch. The dining area, which sits beneath a stunning glass roof, is a popular spot for residents to see and be seen. Afternoon tea is a tradition here, as are dry martinis at the bar, a more casual affair.

Average main: NKr265 The Grand Hotel, Karl Johans gt. 31, Sentrum, P 23-21-20-00, www.grand.no.

5.2.3 Coffee and Snacks
1. Tullin's

This student favorite has mismatched seats, dubious-quality artwork in gold frames, and chandeliers that feel too pricey for the setting. In other words, it exudes an appealingly relaxed air. Known for: pizza, burgers, and other comfort foods; always crowded with young people; and quick service.

Tullins gt. 2, Sentrum P 22-20-46-16 www.tullins.no Average main: NKr175 Tullins gt.

2. Pascal

This chic little café provides French-inspired lunch cuisine such as croque monsieur and quiche with broccoli or bacon. There's also a tempting selection of freshly made pastries and sweets. Known for: an array of gluten-free cuisine, a calm ambiance, and courteous service.

NKr190 Henrik Ibsens gt. 36, Sentrum P 22-55-00-20 www.pascal.no.

5.2.4 Nightlife

1. Angst

This tavern boasts neon lights, recycled wood furnishings, and a large backyard for weekend events. On weekends, the eccentric atmosphere and good music draw a crowd, so get here early if you want to party.

Number 11 Torggata, Sentrum.

2. Crowbar and Bryggeri

Oslo's largest microbrewery serves suckling pigs and delicious brews on two floors. A cheerful bearded face guides you through the weekly menu.

Sentrum P 21-38-67-57, Torggata 32 www.crowbryggeri.com.

3. Dubliner Folk Pub

This Irish pub has a cheerful ambiance and a great whisky collection. Sports air weekdays.

Sentrum 28, Rådhusgata, P 22-33-70-05 www.dubliner.no.

4. Einbar

This ancient potato cellar near Sentrum and Kvadvraturen is ideal for winter. The Moroccan-themed restaurant has a big wine selection, comfy sofas, and luxurious rugs.

Sentrum   P22-41-55-55,   Prinsens   gt.18 www.restauranteiner.no/einbar.

5. London pub

You can expect to find good drinks, a relaxed atmosphere, and lots of friendly faces here. This enormous gay bar and club have been accessible to the public since 1979.

Pl. 5, Sentrum P 22-70-87-00 www.londonpub.no (C. J. Hambros).

6. Cafe Sor

This vegetarian afternoon café has rustic tables and stone walls. Berry-filled cocktails, DJs, and live music draw crowds at night.

P 23-65-46-46, Torggata No. 11 www.cafesor.no.

5.2.5 Shopping

1. FWSS

Autumn, Winter, Spring, and Summer. This Norwegian label is distinguished by its uncomplicated approach to fashion. The store's stylish natural stone design in Oslo's Promenaden Fashion District echoes the brand's commitment to simple pieces that construct a wardrobe suitable for all seasons.

P 45-85-10-21 www.fallwinterspringsummer.com Prinsens gt. 22, Sentrum.

2. Mette Møller

This Norwegian women's fashion label features an ultrafeminine aesthetic and a focus on environmentally friendly techniques. It is intended to be both fashionable and long-lasting.

Sentrum P 942-50-011 Prinsens gt. www.mettemoller.no.

3. Norway Designs

If you're a fan of Scandinavian design, this venerable store carries art glass, ceramics, silver, and a wide range of domestic items.

Lille Grensen 7, Sentrum, P 23-11-45-10, www.norwaydesigns.no.

4. David-Andersen

Norway's most famous goldsmith, who has been in business from 1876, is also famed for his exquisite silverwork.

www.david-andersen.no Karl Johans gt. 20, Sentrum P 24-14-88-00.

5. Norway Shop

Norway Shop has 3 outlets behind City Hall on the square. It sells a wide range of sweaters and blanket jackets.

Fridtjof Nansens pl 9, Sentrum P 22-33-41-97 www.norwayshop.com.

6. Tom Wood

This Norwegian lifestyle brand offers a modern perspective on classic jewelry, eyewear, and clothing. It is near to the Promenaden Fashion District.

P 919-06-226 Kirkegata 20, Sentrum tomwoodproject.com.

7. Heyerdahl

This chic jeweler and watchmaker is situated on Karl Johans Gate.

Karl Johans gt. 37B, Sentrum P 22-55-25-25 www.heyerdahl.no.

8. Oslo City

This elegant shopping complex in the city center is your last chance to pick up a few goods before boarding your train at Oslo Central Station.

P 81-54-40-33 oslo-city.steenstrom.no Stenersgaten 1, Sentrum.

5.3 Kvadraturen, Aker Brygge, and Tjuvholmen

Kvadraturen, Oslo's oldest neighborhood. After the town burned down for the 14th time in 1624, King Christian IV renamed it Christiania and transferred it to a safer location near Akershus Fortress. The king ordered stone or brick houses to prevent fires. Kvadraturen means "square township" because of its geometrically organized streets.

Akers Mekaniske Verksted was a huge commercial shipyard on this coast for over a century. Postmodern steel-and-glass buildings dominate the skyline. When it's sunny, families fill the waterfront promenade. Luxury restaurants, shops, and galleries line the sea. Bridges connect it to Tjuvholmen, a quieter area, and Bjørvika, a new district north of the sea and east of the city center.

Finding Your Way Around

Several subway stations—Nationaltheatret, Stortinget, and Jernbanetorget—are within walking distance of this waterfront neighborhood.

5.3.1 Sights

1. Akershus Slott og Festning (Akershus Castle and Fortress)

By 1592, this 1299 stone castle and royal home was a cannon-armed fortification. After several sieges, it decayed. Finally restored in 1899. Summer excursions include its beautiful halls, castle church, royal mausoleum, reception rooms, and banquet halls. The Fortress Trail Map, available at the tourist center or online, lets you explore Akershus Fortress and its lush gardens.

Akershus festning, Sentrum P 23-09-39-17 akershusfestning.no The entry to the Fortress grounds is free, although Akershus Slott costs NKr 100.

2. Tjuvholmen Bystrand

Tjuvholmen Bystrand is more of a park at the end of a pier than a beach. The bravest infants touch the chilly water.

Tjuvholmen Boardwalk 2.

3. Astrup Fearnley Modern Art Museum (Astrup Fearnley Museet)

The privately funded Astrup Fearnley Museum of Modern Art is a municipal landmark across the pedestrian bridge from Aker Brygge. Renzo Piano-designed the waterfront complex with three pavilions under a huge glass roof that mimics a sail, fitting for this former shipbuilding town. Contemporary international art has made the collection famous.

P   22-93-60-60   Strandpromenaden   2,   Tjuvholmen
www.afmuseet.no Closed on Monday.

4. Tjuvholmen Sculpture Park

Renzo Piano built the fanciful Tjuvholmen Sculpture Park near the
Astrup Fearnley Museum of Modern Art. Summer picnickers enjoy
this coastal park.

Strandpromenaden   2,   Tjuvholmen   P22–93–60–60
www.afmuseet.no Free

5.3.2 Restaurants

1. Amazonia by BAR

This Latin-American waterfront eatery draws fashion-conscious
locals on weekends. Nearly as popular is the hip dining area with
long oak tables emphasizing communal dining. Perfect cocktails;
renowned breakfast; Nordic-style tacos and other goodies.

NKr145   Bryggegangen   6,   Tjuvholmen   P   940-02-094
amazoniabybar.no/ Closed Sun. and Mon. Weekday lunches are
not served.

2. Lofoten Fiskerestaurant

This Lofoten Islands-themed Aker Brygge restaurant serves Maine lobster and Greenland shrimp. Its clean, simple decor boasts harbor views and a sunny patio. Seafood platters, fish soup, and patio sitting.

Average main: NKr350 Stranden 75, Aker Brygge P22–83–08–08. www.lofoten-fiskerestaurant.no

3. Gamle Rådhus

If you're in Oslo for one night and want a true dining experience, visit Oslo's oldest restaurant, housed in the city's first town hall from 1641. Its traditional fish and game dishes take advantage of the city's best seasonal produce. Lutefisk, powerful and salty catch, exquisite paneled surroundings, and candles.

Nedre Slottsgt. 1, Sentrum P 22–42–01–07 (normal main) NKr320 www.gamleraadhus.no Sundays are closed.

4. Olivia Tjuvholmen

This beloved family-friendly Italian chain consistently delivers with stunning waterfront views, pleasant furniture, and helpful service. Thanks to blankets and warming lights, you may dine outdoors under elegant parasols in cool weather. Affordable pizzas and pastas; fresh Italian ingredients; lively atmosphere.

Average main: NKr180 Bryggegangen 4, Tjuvholmen P 23–11–54–70 oliviarestauranter.no/#! /restaurant/tjuvholmen

5. Solsiden

Sun-kissed and delicious. Don't ignore this organization. Famous for celebrity sightings, wine by the glass, and delicious desserts.

Akershusstranda 13, Aker Brygge P 22-33-36-30 Average main: NKr330 www.solsiden.no Closed from September-mid-May.

5.3.3 Nightlife

1. BA3

This trendy hangout has four unique bars to suit your every need, and its strange moniker comes from its location. The Terrassebaren is airy and bright, while Inkognito is mysterious thanks to its crimson bar stools.

Location: Bygdy Allé 3, Frogner, Phone: (22-55-11-86), Website: (www.ba3.no).

5.3.4 Shopping

1. Aker Brygge Shopping

This refurbished shipyard is the place to be in Oslo, especially for after-work beers in the summer, since it is a pedestrian paradise with more than 30 high-end retailers and an equal number of expensive pubs and restaurants.

Aker Brygge, Steperagata 2, Phone: (22-)83-26-80 Website: (www.akerbrygge.no)

5.4 Bygdøy

The Bygdøy Peninsula, located southwest of the city center, is home to several of the city's most well-known historical attractions. The Vikingskipshuset, one of Norway's most visited landmarks, is located in this area. Oscarshall Slott Åd, the pink castle hidden among the trees, was formerly a royal vacation residence. Also located in this area is the current summer residence of the royal family, a large white house. The Norsk Folkmuseum and farm is home to an authentic black stave church, perfect for metal fans or devout Christians.

Finding Your Way Around

The metro doesn't come anywhere near this massive peninsula. The ferry from Pier 3 behind City Hall is the most relaxing method to reach Bygdøy, and it runs from May through September. The Folk Museum is a short distance from Dronningen, where you can get off. Bus No. 30 runs year-round, and will get you there in around 10–20 minutes.

5.4.1 Sights

1. Bygdø Kongsgård (Bygdøy Royal Estate)

The Norwegian royal family used this almost 500-acre manor residence and farm, now part of the Norwegian Folk Museum. Horseback riding lessons and barnyard animal petting are available at this organic farm. Count Christian Rantzau erected the king's vacation palace, the manor house, in 1733. Royal visits change hours.

Dronning Biancas vei, Bygdøy P 22–12–37–00 bygdokongsgard.no Closed summer/winter

2. Kon-Tiki Museum (Kon-Tiki Museet)

The museum honors Norway's greatest 20th-century explorer. To support his theory that Polynesians originated in the Americas, Thor Heyerdahl sailed the Kon-Tiki from Peru to Polynesia in 1947. His second boat, the Ra II, tested his claim that a reed boat may have reached the West Indies before Columbus. The museum features a cinema room with Peruvian, Polynesian, and Easter Island antiquities.

3. Norwegian Maritime MuseumNorsk Maritimt Museum (Norwegian Maritime Museum)

Here are Norwegian fishing vessels, paintings of fishermen braving harsh seas, and complex ship models. Outside is the Arctic ship

Gjøa. The Ocean: A Way of Life explores Norway's marine history. The model of the Kvaldor boat (AD 600), a 19th-century armed timber vessel, and a modern tanker are on show.

Bygdøynesvn.37, Bygdøy P 22–12–37–00 marmuseum.no NKr 120

4. Oscarshall Slott (Oscarshall Palace)

In the mid-19th century, King Oscar I had this unusual English Gothic rural palace built. There's a park, fountain, pavilion, and stage. Norwegian artists Adolph Tidemand and Hans Gude designed the interior.

Oscarshallveien, Bygdy P 91-70-23-61 www.royalcourt.no/ Closed on Sundays and Mondays and from October to May.

5.4.2 Restaurants

1. Kafe Villa Grand

This stately villa attracts hikers, history buffs, and gardeners for simple, traditional meals by day (open-faced sandwiches) and heartier meals by night (whole grilled fish). Warm days are great in the garden. A luxurious palace on the river, seasonal meat and game, lavish feasts.

Average main: NKr565 Villa Grand, Huk Aveny 56, Bygdøy P 67–10–99–70 www.sult.no/selskapslokaler/villa-grande Closed Mon.

2. Lanternen

This 1920s ferry waiting room-turned-restaurant is located on a wharf in the fjord. The picturesque patio attracts people in summer. Towering shellfish platters, city views, and exquisite pizzas.

Average main: NKr180 E Huk Aveny 2, Bygdøy P 22–43–78–38 www.restaurantlanternen.no Weekends and winter dinner closed.

5.5 Holmenkollen

Holmenkollen, the hill visible from many sections of the city, is home to the famed ski jump and miles of ski paths. This is the place to go if you want to get the best views in the city. In recent years, there has been an increase in the number of locations to stay and eat.

Finding Your Way Around

Line 1 of the Metro is popular with tourists since it goes to the Holmenkollen ski jump. Trams and buses connect this area to the Sentrum in about 20-30 minutes.

5.5.1 Sights

1. Emanuel Vigeland Museum

Emanuel is a famous artist, but not as famous as his older brother Gustav, who created Vigeland Park. His cheeky, natural, and sexy frescoes make Norwegians blush. Take the T-bane Line 1 from Nationaltheatret Station to Frognerseteren and get off at Slemdal, a hillside Oslo neighborhood. This museum is a hidden gem near Slemdal.

Grimelundsvn.8, Frogner P 22–14–57–88 www.emanuelvigeland.museum.no/museum.htm NKr 80 Mid-May–mid-Sept., Mon.–Sat.

2. Skimuseet i Holmenkollen (Holmenkollen Ski Museum)

This iconic ski jump was first constructed in 1892 and has been repaired many times. The futuristic jump still organizes international contests. The world's oldest ski museum showcases 4,000 years of skiing, and the ski-jump simulator puts you in real jumpers' skis. The museum offers tours.

Kongevn. 5, Holmenkollen P-22–92–32–00 holmenkollen.com NKr 140.

3. Frognerseteren

Cross-country skiing and Sunday hikes usually start or end at this overlook. Every Oslo host takes guests there to see the fjords and city skyline. In a structure from 1891, the viewing area features two restaurants: the local favorite Kafe Seterstua, a self-service sandwich and waffle shop, and the sit-down, special-occasion Restaurant Finstua, which serves Norwegian smoked and salted cuisine. Frognerseteren's rough-hewn timbers depict Norwegian mountain life minutes from Oslo.

www.frognerseteren.no, Holmenkollveien 200.

5.5.2 Restaurants

1. Finstua

Finstua offers panoramic mountain views above Holmenkollen ski jump. This rustic, stylish restaurant provides salted and smoked seafood, game, and more from Norwegian chefs. Luxury dining space; vistas from every table; famous apple cake.

Average main: NKr385 Holmenkollvn. 200, P 22–92–40–40 www.frognerseteren.no, July and August weekdays without lunch.

2. De Fem Stuer

This well-renowned restaurant in the ancient and recently rebuilt Scandic Holmenkollen Park Hotel beside the iconic ski jump delivers excellent food in a stately setting with stunning views over Oslo. Nordic and cosmopolitan cuisines combine traditional and new elements. One of Oslo's most stunning buildings, superb dining room, and award-winning chef.

Average main: NKr350 Scandic Holmenkollen Park Hotel, Kongevn. 26, Holmenkollen P 22–92–20–00 www.scandichotels.com/hotels/norway/oslo/scandic-holmenkollen-park/restaurant-and-bar.

Chapter 6: Oslofjord

6.1 Top Reasons to Visit

Check out some enormous castles: Historic fortifications built to withstand land and sea attacks can be explored in places like Drbak and Halden.

Masterpieces of art: The abundance of world-class museums, enormous contemporary galleries, and artisanal workshops in this otherwise rural area come as no great shock.

Dine and drink by the Fjordside: There are plenty of locally brewed aquavits and beers to go around in addition to the plentiful shellfish platters, freshly caught salmon, and turbot.

You sank my warship: Visit the breathtaking Oscarsborg Festning to learn about the tragic history of the German battleship Blücher.

Enjoy a night in a historic hotel: You won't find any chain hotels in Oslofjord; instead, choose from a wide variety of unique inns, hotels, and villas located on private islands.

Those using the DFDS boat into the Norwegian capital of Oslo will follow the waterway partially via the fjord's massive forked mouth. Many Oslo residents spend their summers in the Oslofjord region, which is located to the south and west of the Norwegian capital. Tourists visit for the region's rich history, which includes Viking monuments, World War II memorials, fortified villages, and artist colonies from the late 19th century.

6.2 Drøbak

South of Oslo by 35 kilometers (21 miles).

Although it is less than half an hour from the capital, the picturesque town of Drøbak, with its colorful wooden cottages and winding cobblestone lanes, gives the appearance of a typical Sørlander (southern) town. Day travelers from Oslo frequently visit Drøbak for the beach and the seafood restaurants. Among the area's most fascinating attractions is Oscarborg Festning, a fortification on a nearby island that tells the terrible story of the German warship Blücher's drowning in the fjord. Bring the kids to view the aquatic inhabitants at Drøbak Akvarium.

6.2.1 Sights

1. Drøbak Akvarium (Drøbak Aquarium)

From Morgan the deep-sea eel to Hugo the catfish, this modest but unique aquarium includes 14 tanks full with fjord species that will thrill kids. Kids may touch manager Klaus Bareksten's colorful starfish in the big basins.

Located at Havnegata 4 and Drøbak P 91-10-84-20; NKr 70.

2. Friluftsmuseet (Open-Air Museum)

The spectacular Follo Museum expansion is hidden in woodland near Drøbak. An open-air exhibition of old Oslofjord houses features regional history and current arts and handicrafts.

Drøbak, Belsjøveien 17, 66–93–66–36 mia.no/follomuseum/friluftsmuseet Closed Mon.

3. Drøbak Båthavna (Drøbak Harbor)

The Little Mermaid in Copenhagen Harbour is famous, but Drøbak Harbor has three mermaids on the rocks. Norwegian artist Reidar Finsrud created the humorous bronze sculpture. The Drøbak Akvarium is nearby.

Drøbak, Havnagata.

4. Drøbak Gjestehavn (Drøbak Marina)

Drøbak Marina, with its fjord vistas, greets many arrivals to this seaside town. The popular restaurant Sjøstjernen is there.

Badehusgata, Drøbak P64–90–60–00

6.2.2 Restaurants

1. Cafe Sjøstjernen

Locals love this spot, whose name translates to "Starfish" in Norwegian, which is conveniently located near Drøbak Gjestehavn. You can see for miles along the fjord from your table, and the modern concrete and glass exterior stands out in the otherwise historic town. No better place to take in the fjord, lively crowds, and regular performances.

Drøbak P 90–75–61–15.

2. Telegrafen

Fire damaged the original building, but old-fashioned carpentry reconstructed it. It matches the original down to the wood trim and wallpaper designs. Beautiful architecture, terrace views of the fjord, and delicious desserts.

Average main: NKr250 Storgata 10, Drøbak P 915–25–359 https://telegrafendrobak.no/.

3. Det Gamle Bageri Ost & Vinstue

This restaurant's name—the Old Bakery, Wine, and Cheese Room—is charming. Salads, sandwiches, and salmon in a sweet-mustard sauce are available early and late. Outdoor tables are popular; music-loving crowd; small but comprehensive food.

Main average: NKr220 Havnebakken 1, Drøbak P 64–93–21–05 www.detgamlebageri.no.

6.2.3 Coffee and Snacks

1. Cafe Drøbak

This beautiful ice cream parlor resembles an Italian gelateria. Pistachio and caramel homemade flavors are made into cones, cups, and sundaes. Good baked pastries, fast lunchtime sandwiches, and alluring display cases.

Average main: NKr25 Drøbak, Torget 3 P 913–18–087.

6.2.4 Shopping

1. Galleri Finsrud

Reidar Finsrud, an artist with white hair and paint-covered dungarees, displays Neoclassical and modern works in his studio and gallery. Ponds and fountains fill a groomed garden. Finsrud City, a model of a moving town, is the highlight. Boats in the harbor, buses speeding through tunnels, and tourists taking photos from a bridge are beautiful elements.

Badeveien 12, Drøbak P 64–93–23–99 www.galleri-finsrud.no Sun closed.

2. Tregaarden's Christmas House (Tregaarden's Julehus)

Eva Johansen's Santa Claus stories keep Drøbak's Christmas going. Johansen convinces kids to write him thousands of letters. She drew and developed many of the gorgeous cards, toys, and ornaments sold here. The town's central square's sparkling shop was erected in 1876 to lodge mariners who couldn't reach Oslo due to the frozen fjord.

Havnebakken 6, Drøbak P 64–93–41–78 julehus.no.

6.3 Son

25 km (15 miles) south of Drøbak

Son (pronounced soon) is a river immediately south of Drøbak where you may go swimming, sailing, and basking in the sun. This vacation town is located in a historic fishing and boating village and has always attracted creative types. Even now, it attracts a large number of artists and, if you're lucky, city dwellers throughout the summer.

Finding Your Way Around

Son, a fishing community on the coast just south of Drøbak, makes for a pleasant diversion. There are other buses that take roughly 40 minutes from Oslo to get here.

6.3.1 Sights

1. Son Kystkultursenter (Son Coastal Culture Center)

The Son Coastal Culture Centre in Son's harbor has a museum on the dock, several beautiful ancient boats in the sea, and a small shop.

Storggata 19, Son P 66-93-66-36 www.facebook.com/SonKystkultursenter Closed on Mondays and from mid-August to mid-May

6.3.2 Restaurants

1. Restaurant Sjoeboden Son

Restaurant Sjoeboden Son, located on the waterfront in a rusty red structure, offers a pleasant dining area with rough-hewn log walls and an outside terrace extending over the sea. There are numerous seafood options, such as steamed mussels with nicely cooked fries. Known for: gorgeous older waterfront building; superb service from start to end; modest menu of local favorites.

Main price: NKr220 Storgata 27, Son P 465-44-811 Closed Mon.

6.4 Fredrikstad

61 kilometers (38 miles) south of Son

The Glomma, Norway's longest river, flows calmly past Norway's oldest fortified city. 1600s bastions and moat. Gamlebyen—the Old Town—has half-timber homes, moats, and drawbridges.

Finding Your Way Around

From Drøbak or Son up the coast (driving is recommended for the short trip) or Oslo (driving down the E6 takes approximately an hour, and a rail from Oslo Central Station takes a few minutes longer), Fredrikstad is simple to reach.

The entertaining, free boat between ancient and new towns is essential. Park well and walk around town.

6.4.1 Sights

1. Fredrikstad Domkirke (Fredrikstad Cathedral)

The 1860 neo-Gothic Fredrikstad Cathedral dominates the city center. It has Emanuel Vigeland stained glass, like Oslo Cathedral.

Riddervoldsgate 5, Fredrikstad P69-95-98-00.

2. Fredrikstad Museum

This tiny museum near the waterfront chronicles the town's development from the 16th century to the present. Kids love whittling old-fashioned toys.

Tøihusgaten 41, Fredrikstad P 69-11-56-50 ostfoldmuseene.no/fredrikstad NKr 80.

6.4.2 Restaurants

1. Big Fish Cafe

Locals, summer visitors, and first-timers appreciate this family-run cafe and brewery. The fish-and-chips and seafood platters aren't greasy or typical. Massive outdoor terrace; great cocktails; pleasant crew.

Average main: NKr220 Torvet 6, Fredrikstad P 69–37–88–00 bigfishcafe.no Closed Mon–Thurs.

2. Majorens Kro

Markus Nagele, an Austrian hunter, angler, and forager, runs this popular seafood and game restaurant. Try its game buffet or catch of the day. Hunting and fishing crowd; large game banquets; near important sites.

Average main: NKr250 Voldportgaten 73, Fredrikstad 69–32–15–55 www.majoren.no.

6.4.3 Shopping

1. Glashütte

Glashütte, a famous glass-blowing studio and business, exhibits and sells in Norwegian galleries. Watch glassblowers make schnapps glasses and beautiful vases. After cooling, the crew will make you a unique keepsake.

Fredrikstad, Torsnesvn. 1, 48–09–52–39 abelsawe@online.no.

6.5 Halden

Located 18 miles (30 km) to the south of Fredrikstad.

Several noteworthy historical sites can be found in this picture-perfect town. Due to border conflicts between Norway and Sweden in the past, fortifications were previously necessary to protect the area along the Swedish border. King Karl XII was killed in 1718 during the most memorable skirmish at Fredriksten stronghold.

Finding Your Way Around

Buses and trains arrive here from Oslo and Fredrikstad, as well as other cities in the vicinity of the water. From Fredrikstad, a trip on the E6 takes around 40 minutes and is a direct route.

6.5.1 Sights

1. Fredriksten Festning (Fredriksten Fortress)

This star-shaped castle was built in the late 1600s to deter Swedish invaders. From the 17th century to World War II, the former jail exhibits its international wars. Bird claws were used in folk medicine in an antique pharmacy. The bakery could feed 5,000 men, and the brewery could quench their thirst with 3,000 liters of beer at the further end of the inner courtyard. If this makes you hungry, visit Fredriksten Kro, an old-fashioned bar with outside seating.

Halden, Generalveien 27, 69–11–56–50 www.visithalden.com.

2. Rød Herregård

Norwegian 18th-century manor Rød Herregård (Red Manor House) is one of the best preserved. A restored structure displays stuffed animal hunting trophies, vintage furniture, and artwork. The fjord side manor has an English and Baroque garden. The home contains a summer-only café, gallery, and weapons collection. From May to September, three guided tours are available daily.

Herregårdsveien 10, Halden P69–11–56–50 www.visitoestfold.com/no/halden/artikler/Rod-Herregard Closed Oct.–Apr.

6.5.2 Restaurants

1. Rekekaféen

Rekekaféen serves fresh fish and seafood near marina sheds on a floating pier. The fishing boats are close enough to touch while enjoying the sea breezes and waterfront vistas. Smoked fish and prawns, huge seafood platters, fish soup.

Main average: NKr250 Strandstredet 4, Halden www.rekekafeen.no Monday and Tuesday are closed.

6.6 Baerum

13 kilometers (8 miles) west of Oslo.

Bærum, a trendy Oslo suburb, is 20 minutes away. The lovely Bærums Verk is located on the Lomma River in a residential neighborhood. The Bærums Verk iron foundry owners restored their industrial town in the 1960s. Today, people flock to its charming stores, workshops, and shows. The workers' cramped wooden houses on Verksgata may be seen as you explore the reconstructed settlement. The doors arc in the back in case a fire from the works spilled through the main street. Then there's Henie Onstad, known as the "MoMA" of Oslofjord.

6.6.1 Sights
1. Museum of Baerums Verk

This museum houses a large collection of cast-iron ovens made at Bærums Verk, dating from the 18th century to the mid-20th century when the facility closed. English tours are available.

P 67-13-00-18 Verksgata 15, Bærums Verk www.baerumsverk.no.

6.6.2 Restaurants

1. Vaertshuset Bærums Verk

Værtshuset (meaning "The Inn"), Norway's oldest restaurant, is a must-see on any itinerary that includes the neighboring ironworks. The inn first opened its doors in 1640 and was a popular stop on the King's Road between Oslo and Bergen. Known for: wild game such as venison, lovely dining room, and great service.

Average main: NKr665 Vertshusveien 10, Brums Verk P 67-80-02-00 www.vaertshusetbaerum.no.

6.7 Vollen

14 kilometers (9 miles) southwest of Baerum.

This town boasts a picturesque harbor with views of the fjord. It's a wonderful stopover if you're touring the coast. This quaint village is filled with art galleries, boutiques, and seafood restaurants that don't try to outdo each other (unlike some of the larger towns in the Fjord region).

Finding Your Way Around

Getting to Vollen from Oslo is quickest via train, which takes only 20 minutes. It adds around 10 minutes to the trip time if you drive there alone or use a bus.

6.7.1 Sights

1. Oslofjordmuseet (Oslofjord Museum)

Impressive, engaging, amusing, and instructive for everyone. The Oslofjord Museum has grown from a vast collection of wooden vessels. The country's nautical history, beach culture, and boatbuilding history are all here.

Chr. Jensens Vei 8, Vollen P 406–06–635 mia.no/oslofjordmuseet Closed Mon.

6.7.2 Restaurants

1. Vito's Restaurant

This cheerful, family-run beachfront restaurant serves lasagna with a substantial beef sauce and fresh mussels with fries. The Sicilian chef's diversified menu emphasizes Sicilian inspirations and fresh vegetables. Waterfront location with plenty of outdoor sitting; elegant design; great bar.

Average main: NKr250 Slemmestadveien 416, Vollen P 66–79–89–95 www.vitosrestaurant.no.

Chapter 7: Southern Norway

7.1 Top Reasons to Visit

Hike Preikestolen: Towering Pulpit Rock is one of Norway's most famous treks, with stunning vistas at the end.

Discover Kristiansand: Wander the picturesque streets of the "capital of southern Norway," where you'll never run out of historical attractions to see.

Relax in seaside towns: In picturesque waterfront settlements like Kragerø and Sandefjord, you'll rub shoulders with vacationing Norwegians.

In Stavanger, dig deep: This vibrant city has an interesting history and is home to Northern Europe's largest and best-preserved collection of wooden dwellings.

Explore the Lysefjord: This gorgeous waterway, one of Norway's most popular locations, shows treasures such as the gravity-defying Kjerag Boulder.

Oslo locals go to the warm southern coast in summer. With a warm summer climate and landscape ranging from inland mountains and forests to coastal flatland, southern Norway is a great escape for nature lovers. Kristiansand, Sandefjord, and Lillesand are tourist towns on Norway's Riviera, the southern coast of the country. However, charming seaside villages, busy harbors full of fishing boats, and colorful 18th- and 19th-century wooden buildings dot the countryside.

7.2 Sandefjord

South of Oslo, 124 kilometers (77 miles).

Since the 1800s, Norwegians—particularly Oslo residents—have visited Sandefjord as a spa. Today, the city still relies on trading and whaling. It can be congested, especially in summer, but it has fantastic seafood restaurants and boat tours around the coast.

Finding Your Way Around

Vestfoldbanen trains and buses connect Sandefjord to Oslo multiple times a day. From Oslo, E18 takes 90 minutes across the municipality.

7.2.1 Sights

1. Bryggekapellet

Bryggekapellet, Europe's only floating church, welcomes visitors to light a candle or listen to the waves. Open 6 weeks each summer.

Brygga 1, Sandefjord Vestfold Telemark P33–47–62–52 sandefjord.kirken.no Closed Sept.–May.

2. Hvalfangstmonumentet (Whaling Monument)

This Knut Steen sculpture is a Sandefjord icon, surrounded by beautiful water plumes. It's impressive that the monument revolves.

Hvalfangstmonumentet, Indre Havn, Vestfold og Telemark.

7.2.2 Restaurants

1. La Scala

This restaurant is floating off the dock, giving you vistas in all directions. Its maritime-themed windows can be opened to catch summer breezes. Perfect setting; fireplace warms cool nights; pleasant environment year-round.

Average main: NKr300 Brygga 5, Sandefjord Vestfold og Telemark P 33–46–15–90 www.la-scala.no.

7.3 Kragerø

Norwegians dream of owning a hytte (cabin). Kragerø's main street is a waterway where boaters dock and dine at one of the many outstanding restaurants.

Finding Your Way Around

E18 to Gjerdemyra from Oslo or Kristiansand. Local Route 38 leads to Kragerø's center. Several boats leave Kragerø for the archipelago's larger islands. Neslandsvatn Station in Drangedal is the closest bus stop.

7.3.1 Sights

1. Jomfruland Nasjonalpark (Jomfruland National Park)

Jomfruland National Park, accessible by ferry from Kragerø, is an excellent way to see the archipelago and its creatures. The 2016 117-square-km (45-square-mile) protected area comprises Jomfruland and Stråholmen. The park contains 98% ocean. Sand dunes have microscopic critters, so watch your step.

Kragerø Vestfold og Telemark www.jomfrulandnasjonalpark.no.

2. Kittelsenhuset (Kittelsen House)

Norwegian artist Theodor Kittelsen's Kragerø childhood home is a museum. Most Norwegians remember his children's book and fairy tale illustrations.

Th. Kittelsens Vei 5, Kragerø Vestfold og Telemark P 35–54–45–00 www.telemarkmuseum.no/kittelsenhuset NKr 100 Closed Mon.

7.3.2 Restaurants

1. Skåtøy Kafe

Skåtøy Kafe, on Skåtøy Island, is 10 minutes by boat from Kragerø. Friendly staff, outdoor sitting, and a cozy setting. Fish soup, wine, summer hours.

Average main: NKr200 Stoppedalveien 2, Skåtøy Island Vestfold og Telemark P 92–04–33–14 www.skatoykafe.no Closed Sept.–May.

7.4 Risør

234 kilometers (145 miles) southwest of Oslo and 51 kilometers (32 miles) southwest of Kragerø.

Risør is a lovely seaside community with a long history of boatbuilding, and it is one of the best-preserved wooden towns in Europe.

Finding Your Way Around

The driving time for the car from Oslo to Risør is under three hours. Go-Ahead's Sørtoget connects Oslo and Kristiansand and stops at the closest station, Gjerstad. The closest train station to Risør is Gjerstad Station, which is 35 kilometers (22 miles) away.

7.4.1 Sights

1. Risør Akvarium

Risør Akvarium, the only saltwater aquarium in southern Norway, is home to more than 500 species of fish and marine animals. The largest lobster in Norway is a big hit with the kids, and they also like feeding the fish.

P 41-64-87-59, Strandgate 14, Risør Agder www.risorakvarium.no, NKr 120, weekdays closed.

2. Risør Fiskemottak

This market is conveniently located near both fishing trawlers and storage buildings, so fishermen can easily bring their daily catch to sell. The name "fish landing," or "Fiskemottak," tells it all. There are likely to be fish species you have never seen before. In addition to the restaurant, there is a fish market.

Solsiden 3, Risør Agder, P 37-15-23-50 www.fiskemottaket.no.

7.4.2 Restaurants

1. Stangholmen Fyr (Stangholmen Lighthouse Restaurant)

This summer-only lighthouse restaurant serves fresh local seafood and fish. The modest white clapboard building on the cliff has shutters for bad weather. Known for: excellent seafood, well-prepared steaks, and an enjoyable adventure.

Average main: NKr350 Stangholmen Fyr, Risør Agder P 900–93–400 www.stangholmen.no Closed mid-August–mid-June.

7.5 Arendal

259 kilometers (161 miles) southwest of Oslo; 49 kilometers (30 miles) southwest of Risør.

The wooden buildings' flower boxes in Arendal's Tyholmen (Old Town) spill pink and scarlet flowers. The small lanes off the waterfront are attractive in this town. Visit the 1815 town hall.

Norway's tallest timber building features around 300 portraits, primarily by local artists from the 19th century.

Finding Your Way Around

Arendal is south of Oslo. E18 takes 3 hours and 20 minutes to drive. Vy operates frequent Oslo buses.

7.5.1 Sights

1. Bomuldsfabriken

The rebuilt Bomuldsfabriken (Cotton Factory) produced cotton flannel clothes from 1898 to 1960, making it an interesting gallery space. Today, it features changing art exhibits as well as a permanent collection of 35 paintings by some of Norway's most prominent artists.

P 37-01-30-60 Oddenveien 5, Arendal Agder www.bomuldsfabriken.no Closed on Monday.

2. Kuben Arendal

This museum, founded in 1832, houses a wonderful collection of antiques relating to coastal life, ranging from toys to farm tools. Learn about the 1767 slave ship Fredensborg and the region's folk art traditions.

P 37-01-79-00 www.kubenarendal.no Parkveien 16, Arendal Agder P 37-01-79-00 Closed on Monday.

7.5.2 Restaurants

1. Egon Arendal

Egon provides high-quality Norwegian classics. The dining room and street deck are comfortable at this restaurant. Family-friendly; patio seating; delicious appetizers.

Average main: NKr250 Thon Hotel Arendal, Friergangen 1, Arendal   Agder   P   37–05–21–72 www.egon.no/restauranter/arendal.

Chapter 8: Bergen

8.1 Top Reasons to Visit

Stroll near the water's edge: Bergen's colorful wooden dock structures are a must-see and a designated UNESCO World Heritage Site.

Travel the Fløibanen by air: The ride on the funicular from the city streets to the mountain's peak overlooking the fjord takes only seven minutes.

Something at the Fisketorget: The Bergen Fish Market, which has been there since the 1200s, is one of the busiest and most well-known open-air markets in all of Norway.

Expedition to Troldhaugen: Visit the grand home where Bergen's favorite son, composer Edvard Grieg, created many of his best-known works.

Decipher the KODE: There are several fantastic museums with collections spanning the ages scattered around the shore of Lake Lille Lungegårdsvann.

Bergen is Norway's second-largest city, and many tourists instantly fall in love with it. It is a magical town because of its seven rounded, verdant mountains, pastel wood cottages, old pier, winding cobblestone alleyways, and Hanseatic artifacts. In addition to "Trebyen" (Wooden City) and "Regnbyen" (Rainy City; named for the average of 260 days of annual precipitation), it is also known as "Fjordbyen" (gateway to the fjords).

8.2 Bryggen

Olav Kyrre founded commercial Bergen in 1070. Bergen became one of the four Hanseatic commerce centers in the 14th century. Bryggen's Hanseatic timber buildings have triangular cookie-cutter roofs and are painted red, blue, yellow, and green. The buildings' shops, cafés, and museums draw tourists and locals. These modest houses, the stocky Rosenkrantz Tower, the Fløyen, and the yachts lining the pier are reflected in the harbor's waters in the evening when the Bryggen is illuminated, creating one of northern Europe's most beautiful cityscapes.

Vågsbunnen, south of the city, is a lively and diverse neighborhood. Many trendy pubs, clubs, and designer boutiques are located here.

8.2.1 Sights

1. Bergen Domkirke (Bergen Cathedral)

The cathedral's varied architecture reflects its stormy past. 13th-century Gothic choir and lower towers are the oldest. The tower wall has a 1665 bullet from an English-Dutch conflict in Bergen harbor. Organ concerts are a great way to enjoy the cathedral.

Domkirke gt., Bryggen P 55–59–32–73

2. Bryggens Museum

This museum has medieval artifacts. Reconstructed dwelling rooms and relics like tools and shoes show Bergen at its peak in 1300. Bergen was Norway's capital, the largest town, and the cosmopolitan commercial center.

Dreggsallmenningen 3, Bryggen P55–30–80–30 www.bymuseet.no/en NKr 100.

3. Fløibanen (Mount Fløyen Funicular)

Mt. Fløyen, the most accessible of Bergen's seven summits, offers a stunning perspective of the city and its suburbs. The funicular rises 320 meters (1,050 feet) above sea level in eight minutes. Cars leave every 30 minutes. A café, shop, and playground are on top. Walk back downtown or hike up Ulriken, Bergen's tallest mountain.

Vetrlidsalmenningen 21, Bryggen P 55–33–68–00 www.floyen.no/en/ NKr 65 each way.

4. Lille Øvregaten

The lovely "Little Upper Street" is one of the city's oldest. These 19th-century clapboard buildings on a rough cobblestone street show Bergen 100 years ago.

Bryggen, Lille Øvregaten

8.2.2 Restaurants

1. Bryggeloftet & Stuene

The pleasant dining area contains a fireplace, oil paintings of the city's maritime history and wooden display cabinets with model ships and other relics. Norwegian country food is served. Monkfish, venison, and reindeer fillets in cream sauce are recommended. Best fish soup in Bryggen; nice location; big portions.

Average main: NKr350 Bryggen 11, P 55–30–20–70 Visit www.bryggeloftet.no.

2. Enhjørningen

This town's best seafood restaurant is named after the unicorn on its old wooden doorway. Enhjørningen's menu, which varies daily, is modern Norwegian. Steamed halibut and other local seafood; modernized classic recipes; waterfront location.

Average main: NKr360 Enhjørningsgården 29, Bryggen P 55–30–69–50 www.enhjorningen.no Sun. Sept.–mid-May. No lunch.

3. Taperia Tapas & Pinxos

Seafood, cheese, cured cold cuts, and pintxos—authentic Spanish cuisine. Two-story Skostredet sitting area.

Average main: NKr250 Skostredet 1b, Downtown www.taperia.no/.

4. 26 North

One of Bryggen's greatest restaurants has a stunning glass ceiling in its main dining area. A deck is available on warm evenings. Best New Nordic cooking; wonderful location in Bryggen; nice outdoor deck.

Average main: NKr 325 Radisson Blu Hotel Bryggen, Bryggen 47 P 477–10–467 www.26north.no/bergen/ No dinner Fri., Sat.

5. Villani

This traditional trattoria smells like wood-fired pizza as you enter. Homemade pasta is another specialty. Known for: corner location on busy Skostredet; large assortment of hand-picked Italian wines; quiet dining room.

Average main: NKr259 Skostredet 9a, Vågsbunnen P 55–31–55–55 www.villani.no.

8.2.3 Coffee and Snacks

1. Godt Brød

Delicious cinnamon buns (of several types) and open-faced sandwiches are baked fresh to order at this renowned organic bakery. Vegan friendly, uses only organic products, and makes great grab-and-go meals.

Nkr150 at Nedre Korskirkeallmenningen 12, Vågsbunnen, Phone: 55-32-80-00, Website: www.godtbrod.no.

8.2.4 Nightlife

1. Baklommen Bar

This cozy cocktail lounge may be found in one of the warped ancient buildings on the dock, and its ceiling is supported by Y-shaped beams.

Address: Enhjørningsgården 29, Bryggen P: 55:32:27:47 Website: www.tokokker.no/baklommen-bar No Sunday or Monday Hours.

2. Bar 3

At the chill Bar 3, you may play various games like shuffleboard, Ping-Pong, and pinball. There's a fun variety of beers to try, and you and your pals will have plenty of room to disperse.

3 Rosenkrantzgt., Bryggen, P 488-89-200; website: http://bar3.no/.

8.2.5 Shopping

1. Berle Bryggen

Find authentic Norwegian knitwear and souvenirs, including the full Dale of Norway range of sweaters and cardigans, trolls, pewter, down duvets, and more.

Bryggen P 55-10-95-00, Bryggen 5 Closed on Sundays www.berlebryggen.com.

2. Ting Bergen

You can shop for yourself, your family, and your house and find high-quality designer goods at reasonable prices. You can find a thoughtful present here.

Bryggen 13, Bryggen P 55–21–54–80 www.ting.no/ting-i-bergen-1.

3. Oleana

The flagship store of this well-known Norwegian design brand is stocked with beautiful garments and fabrics featuring both classic and modern Norwegian designs.

Bryggen P 55-31-05-20, Strandkaien 2A www.oleana.no Closed on Sundays.

4. Råvarene

This innovative store sells sustainable and reusable items to help people lead more zero-waste lives.

Located at Marken 9, Vågsbunnen, phone: +47 930-64-6960, website: http://raavarene.com/, closed: Sunday.

Conclusion

Norway is an amazing travel destination with a wide variety of sights to see and activities to partake in. The country has a breathtaking landscape full of breathtaking fjords, glaciers, and mountains. Hiking, skiing, and dog sledding are just a few of the exciting activities available to visitors, who can also choose to simply relax in a peaceful setting.

Cities in Norway, such as Oslo, Bergen etc., exhibit an ideal synthesis of contemporary culture and long-standing customs. Tourists may enjoy wonderful Norwegian cuisine while visiting exciting art scenes and historic landmarks. Viking history and culture provide a fascinating dimension to any visit to the land.

The Northern Lights are genuinely magical phenomena that bring visitors from all over the world to the Arctic to observe their dancing across the night sky. The summer months in Norway are especially special because of the Midnight Sun when sunshine lasts nearly 24 hours, and there are countless opportunities for outdoor activities.

Norwegians are some of the friendliest people you'll ever meet, and their dedication to responsible tourism guarantees that future generations will be able to appreciate the country's natural splendor just as much as you do. Norway is a fantastic destination for those interested in the outdoors, learning about the country's rich history, or just relaxing.

Norway can be an expensive vacation spot, so it's best to start saving early. The memories and insights gained from traveling across this lovely country are, nonetheless, invaluable. Get ready for an experience of a lifetime as you explore Norway's stunning landscapes. You'll be welcomed with open arms in Norway.

Made in United States
North Haven, CT
24 July 2023